Careers in the Investment World

The Basic Investor's Library

Chelsea House Publishers

Careers in the Investment World

RACHEL S. EPSTEIN

Paul A. Samuelson
Senior Editorial Consultant

CHELSEA HOUSE PUBLISHERS   New York   New Haven   Philadelphia

Editor-in-Chief   Nancy Toff
Executive Editor   Remmel T. Nunn
Managing Editor   Karyn Gullen Browne
Copy Chief   Juliann Barbato
Picture Editor   Adrian G. Allen
Art Director   Giannella Garrett
Manufacturing Manager   Gerald Levine

Staff for   CAREERS IN THE INVESTMENT WORLD
Senior Editor   Marjorie P. K. Weiser
Associate Editor   Andrea E. Reynolds
Copyeditor   Michael Goodman
Associate Picture Editor   Juliette Dickstein
Picture Researcher   Cheryl Moch
Senior Designer   Laurie Jewell
Designers   Barbara Bachman, Jairo Botero, Laurence Ian Burns
Production Coordinator   Laura McCormick

Creative Director   Harold Steinberg

Contributing Editor   Robert W. Wrubel
Consulting Editor   Shawn Patrick Burke

3   5   7   9   8   6   4   2
Library of Congress Cataloging in Publication Data

Epstein, Rachel S.
  Careers in the investment world.

  (The Basic investor's library)
  Bibliography: p.
  Includes index.
  1. Investments—Vocational guidance.   2. Finance—
Vocational guidance.   I. Title.   II. Series
HG4528.E67   1987   332.6'023   87-13182
ISBN 1-55546-631-1

CONTENTS

Learning the Tools of Investing

PAUL A. SAMUELSON

When asked why the great financial house of Morgan had been so successful, J. Pierpont Morgan replied, "Do you suppose that's because we take money seriously?"

Managing our personal finances is a serious business, and something we all must learn to do. We begin life dependent on someone else's income and capital. But after we become independent, it is a remorseless fact of nature that we must not only support ourselves for the present but must also start saving money for retirement. The best theory of saving that economists have is built upon this model of *life-cycle saving*: You must provide in the long years of prime working life for what modern medicine has lengthened to, potentially, decades of retirement. This life-cycle model won a 1985 Nobel Prize for my MIT colleague Franco Modigliani, and it points up the need to learn the rudiments of personal finance.

Learning to acquire wealth, however, is only part of the story. We must also learn to avoid losing what we have acquired. There is an old saying that "life insurance is *sold*, not bought." The same goes for stocks and bonds. In each case, the broker is guaranteed a profit, whether or not the customer benefits from the transaction. Knowledge is the customer's only true ally in the world of finance. Some gullible victims have lost their lifetime savings to unscrupulous sales promoters. One chap buys the Brooklyn Bridge. Another believes a stranger who asserts that gold will quickly double in price, with no risk of a drop in value. Such "con" (confidence) rackets get written up in the newspapers and on the police blotters every day.

I am concerned, however, about something less dramatic than con artists; something that is not at all illegal, but that costs ordinary citizens a thousand times more than outright embezzlement or fraud. Consider two families, neighbors who could be found in any town. They started alike. Each worked equally hard, and had about the same income. But the Smiths have to make do with half of what the Joneses have in retirement income, for one simple reason: The Joneses followed prudent practice as savers and investors, while the Smiths tried to make a killing and constantly bought and sold stocks at high commissions.

The point is, it does matter to learn how financial markets work, and how you can participate in them to your best advantage. It is important to know the difference between *common* and *preferred* stocks, between *convertible* and *zero-coupon* bonds. It is not difficult to find out what mutual funds are, and to understand the difference between the successful Fund A, which charges no commission, or "load," and the equally successful Fund B, which does charge the buyer such a fee.

All investing involves risk. When I was a young assistant professor, I said primly to my great Harvard teacher, Joseph Schumpeter: "We should speculate only with money we can afford to lose." He gently corrected me: "Paul, there is no such money. Besides, a speculator is merely an investor who has lost." Did Schumpeter exaggerate? Of course he did, but in the good cause of establishing the basic point of financial management: Good past performance is no guarantee of the future.

That is why *diversification* is the golden rule. "Don't put all your eggs in one basket. And watch all those baskets!" However, diversification does not mean throwing random darts at the financial pages of the newspaper to choose the best stocks in which to invest. The most diversified strategy of all would be to invest in a portfolio containing all the stocks in the comprehensive Standard & Poor's 500 Stock Index. But rather than throw random darts at the financial pages to pick out a few stocks, why not throw a large bath towel at the newspaper instead? Buy a bit of everything in proportion to its value in the larger world: Buy more General Motors than Ford, because GM is the bigger company; buy General Electric as well as GM because the auto industry is just one of many industries. That is called being an *index investor*. Index investing makes sense because 70 out of 100 investors who try to do better than the Standard & Poor's 500, the sober record shows, do worse over a 30-year period.

Do not take my word for this. The second lesson in finance is to be skeptical of what writers and other experts say, and that includes being skeptical of professors of economics. So I wish readers *Bon voyage!* on their cruise to command the fundamentals of investing. On your mainship flag, replace the motto "Nothing ventured, nothing gained" with the Latin words *Caveat emptor*—Let the buyer beware.

Careers in the Investment World

The world of investments is an exciting place to work. It is filled with energy and growing rapidly. From 1976 to 1986 the number of people employed in this industry more than doubled, from 176,800 to 403,800. In the same period the value of all stocks listed on the New York Stock Exchange has also followed suit, rising to $2,199,258,000,000 (that is, more than $2 trillion worth).

One reason for the growth is the increase in the number of shares of stock bought and sold. In the early 1980s 25 million shares of stock were traded during an ordinary day on the New York Stock Exchange. By the late 1980s, 150-million-share days had become the norm.

The investment industry offers many kinds of jobs, in a variety of organizations. Among the most important employers are companies that deal with securities, primarily stocks and bonds.

WHO SHOULD WORK IN THE INVESTMENT INDUSTRY?

Industry growth means career opportunities, especially for young people. The investment industry is changing, and a changing environment welcomes young people with energy and new ideas.

Some of the changes are due to the creation of different types of investments: Creative investment bankers and brokerage firms constantly devise new products in which people can invest. Other changes concern the people on Wall Street. There was a time when the investment community was built as much on family connections and "old school ties" as on talent. "Whom you knew" was more important than "what you knew." People who worked on Wall Street were almost all male and educated at the "right" prep schools and colleges. In recent years Wall Street firms have searched more widely to find employees with drive and talent. People who want to work on Wall Street should have bachelor's degrees from top undergraduate colleges and/or master's degrees from major graduate schools of business. People with majors in economics and those who are used to working with computers are particularly desirable candidates for many jobs. A good college is important, but the schools that today's investment industry employees have attended are many and varied.

Women did not work full time on the floor of the New York Stock Exchange until 1976. Since then the presence of women has become increasingly evident in the investment industry. In 1976 women held only 36 percent of investment industry jobs; in 1986 women held 46 percent of the jobs and were becoming a noticeable presence at the executive level.

You don't have to work *on* Wall Street to have a "Wall Street" career. There are jobs not only at firms that must be near the major stock exchanges, but also at firms throughout the country that help investors invest, help companies find investors, and that provide the specialized services needed by others in the investment community.

The investment world is a good place to be if you are strongly motivated by money. Compensation is high, and you will be surrounded by people who share your drive. If the securities markets are doing well, intelligent, hard-working, aggressive people can often earn more than $100,000 a year. But the investment business is cyclical: Earnings may go up and down, with a stretch of good years followed by some that are not so good. When the markets do poorly, some people lose their jobs and others earn less money. The survivors know they must wait out the slump and build toward the next upturn of the cycle.

The branch office of a national brokerage firm in Charlotte, North Carolina.

Wall Street is an exciting place to work. People who work there and in similar locations across the country and around the world are a special breed. They speak in short-hand phrases and jargon. Their pace is fast. They thrive on tension and excitement. They are confident and aggressive. When times are good, they are extremely well rewarded. It is a world open to people who have the will to succeed. This book should help you decide if it is the world for you.

What Are the Jobs?

This book describes the work of some of the key people in the financial world—account executives, sales assistants, equities traders, operations department personnel, bond traders, securities analysts, investment bankers, and financial analysts. These are the people who help investors buy and sell stock, who study investment possibilities and recommend investment opportunities, who help companies find investors, and who facilitate sales and manage the vast

The London Stock Exchange.

quantity of record keeping that accompanies investment transactions. These are not the only positions in the investment industry, but they are jobs that are found *only* in this industry.

Some Wall Street jobs are found elsewhere as well. Lawyers, certified public accountants, computer programmers and other specialists, economists, journalists and public relations people, and others provide essential services to the investment industry. Journalists, writers, and editors, for example, produce annual reports; report on financial news in industry publications or in the business sections of newspapers and news magazines; and provide information about and create publications explaining investment products to both the industry and the public.

Where Are the Jobs?

Investment activities occur around the world as well as in the major and regional exchanges within the United States. Tokyo is a major financial center, and London, which was the center of the investment world before World War I, is important once again. Canada, Hong Kong, Italy, West Germany, Mexico, Australia and other nations have important stock exchanges as well. In each of these countries there are jobs directly connected to the markets themselves, as well as within the various firms that interact with the exchange's activities. In addition, jobs can be found at regional and specialty investment firms and in the branch offices of major firms located throughout the country.

But Wall Street still plays the leading role in this theater. The combined value of stocks traded on the Tokyo and London exchanges is less than three-quarters that of shares traded on the New York and American Stock Exchanges in New York. Outside of that city, with a few exceptions, investment firms are generally less competitive, less selective in hiring, and less generous with salaries and commissions. They also tend to be oriented to local concerns and industries, and they encourage employees to become involved in community affairs in ways that New York firms do not. For millions of people these companies are the local "stores" for buying and selling stock.

Careers in the investment industry can be found in brokerage houses, investment and commercial banks, insurance companies, mutual fund companies, credit-rating organizations, and business publications. They also exist in the pension and investment departments of labor unions, government agencies, and many large business organizations.

Traders on the floor of the Financial Futures Market in the Royal Exchange in London. There are investment career opportunities throughout the world.

Brokerages There are about 10 national brokerage houses and a number of regional firms. The larger firms do more research and have investment banking and block trading departments. Brokerages hire large numbers of account executives, sales assistants, operations people, and (except for discount brokerages) securities analysts. All brokerages work through branch offices, which hire the account executives and some operations people. Securities analysts, traders, and investment bankers work at the main office. Most operations people work in or near the headquarters city, usually in a somewhat less prestigious location than the executives of the firm.

MAJOR NATIONAL BROKERAGE FIRMS
Drexel Burnham Lambert *Incorporated*
E. F. Hutton & Company Inc.
Merrill Lynch & Co., Inc.
Paine Webber *Incorporated*
Shearson Lehman Brothers Inc.
Smith Barney, Harris Upham & Co. *Incorporated*
Thomson McKinnon Securities Inc.
Dean Witter Reynolds Inc.

MAJOR INVESTMENT BANKING FIRMS
Bear, Stearns & Co. Inc.
Dillon, Read & Co. Inc.
The First Boston Corporation
Goldman, Sachs & Co.
Kidder, Peabody & Co. *Incorporated*
Morgan Stanley & Co. *Incorporated*
Salomon Brothers Inc.
Wertheim, Schroder & Co., Inc.

WORKING IN
INVESTMENTS

Investment Banking Firms In addition to investment bankers, investment banks hire traders (who serve as account executives for major clients), financial analysts, securities analysts, and operations people. Although there are a few national firms headquartered outside of New York City—Hambrecht & Quist in San Francisco and Alex. Brown in Baltimore—most large-scale investment banking takes place in Manhattan.

Commercial Banks Commercial banks deal with investments through trust departments and investment-banking departments. Trusts are assets from the estates of individuals who have specified in their wills that certain monies are to be "held in trust," that is, managed according to the terms of the will by a trustee, usually a bank, on behalf of the beneficiaries. The trust departments of commercial banks invest for large corporate pension funds as well as for trusts. The banks hire securities analysts to advise them on such investments.

Some banks also have investment banking departments that underwrite government and municipal bonds, offer advice on mergers and acquisitions, and arrange private placements (the sale of stock to a small group of sophisticated investors).

Commercial banks hire traders to increase the value of the money they manage. Banks also have operations departments to process their transactions. Trust, investment banking, and operations departments are located throughout the country at the headquarters of large banks. Almost all trading, however, is done in New York City.

Insurance Companies Insurance companies hire securities analysts to advise them on investing the vast amounts of money they receive. They also hire operations people to process immense amounts of paperwork. Insurance companies tend to be fairly secure workplaces. They are likely to be located outside of New York City; many have headquarters in Hartford, Connecticut.

The equities trading floor in the New York City world headquarters office of Paine Webber.

Mutual Funds   Companies offering mutual funds (an investment in which shareholders' money is pooled and invested in the stocks and bonds of a variety of corporations and other organizations) hire salespeople, whose work is similar to that of account executives. They also hire securities analysts and operations department personnel.

Other Employers   Securities analysts are hired by credit-rating services, such as Standard & Poor's Corporation, Moody's Investors Service, and Dun & Bradstreet. Financial publications, such as *The Value Line Investment Survey*, *Fortune*, and *Business Week*, also employ securities analysts. These publications, as well as a number of individual companies, employ business and financial writers to communicate the information provided by the analysts. There are also small firms, known as *boutiques*, that specialize in securities research and hire analysts to make oral and written presentations. The services provided by these organizations are available to the investment community.

ACCOUNT EXECUTIVE

An account executive, or AE, as stockbrokers are called today, is the person who sells investments to institutions and individuals. These investments include *stocks* (ownership shares in corporations, also known as *equity*) and *bonds* (which represent loans to corporations or government agencies). Account executives may also sell many other types of investments or products.

In most of these transactions the AE acts as an intermediary or broker to make possible buying and selling between two individuals or institutions who never meet and do not know each other's names. Here's how it works: On a certain day, B decides to sell 100 shares of a leading computer company and A wants to buy 100 shares of the same company. A and B each give instructions to their respective broker, who then arranges the transaction. The actual trade is done by traders on the floor of the stock exchange where the computer company is listed.

Account executives are employed mostly by large brokerage houses. Because the activity of AEs generates their income, they are constantly active and spend more than 90 percent of the day on the telephone advising clients and potential clients about what to buy and sell.

Advantages and Disadvantages Account executives cite two main advantages to their jobs. First, once they are established and have a client list acceptable to their firm, their own efforts determine their success to a large extent. Second, they are their own bosses, which means they can make their own working hours and choose the length of time of their vacations. But there are also disadvantages. First, because of the incredible pressure to produce results, in each call to a client or potential client the AE must be fully alert, enthusiastic, knowledgeable, and friendly; there is no time to give in to bad moods on the job. Second, after an initial period, there is no salary. This means that whenever the AE is not working, whether because of illness or a vacation, there is no money being earned. Third, when clients do not invest, an AE's income drops sharply. At times like these, and generally when the market is falling, an AE can become depressed. When stock prices tumble, AEs lose confidence in their ability to pick stocks. Their customers become afraid to invest, and even the effort to generate business becomes difficult. Also, an AE cannot control all aspects of the job. For instance, if stock prices go down, or if the firm's analysts provide bad advice, the AEs may get poor results.

Compensation New AEs generally receive a salary during their first year or two on the job. In some firms, new AEs may also be paid for each new client, or account, they bring to the firm. After the first or second year, AEs receive commissions based on every purchase or sale handled for a client. An AE who generates a lot of activity can earn as much as or more than $100,000 a year. The average AE *payout* (what the AE actually receives as income) is 30 to 35 percent of the firm's commission. Commissions charged to investors are figured as a percentage of the money involved in the transaction. If the firm receives $100 as a commission, then an AE's 30 percent payout will be $30. However, some investments pay higher commissions than others, and payouts can vary from firm to firm. The trend now is to give AEs who produce big commissions for their firms a higher percentage, and to penalize those who are less productive by paying them a smaller percentage of the commissions they generate. The range is from 30 percent to 50 percent.

Qualifications and Training Although most beginning brokers have a college degree and some sales experience, the job has no specific requirements of academic or work experience. A recruiter for one major Wall Street firm says he looks for people who have a history of success, including some leadership positions, to demonstrate initiative and persuasive ability. They should be intelligent, absolutely honest, and understand that 18 out of 20 people they approach will say "no."

There are two prerequisites for becoming a broker who places orders to buy and sell stock: A person must have been employed by a brokerage firm for four months and must have passed a six-hour examination given by the National Association of Securities Dealers, Inc. This organization regulates aspects of the securities industry for the benefit of investors. The test is offered nationwide on the last Saturday of every month. A score of 70 percent is passing, and about three-quarters of those taking the test at any one time pass it.

Training for the examination, as well as for selling investments after passing it, consists of on-the-job observation and listening, learning from books, and attending for-

Emil L. Chen, an account executive (or stockbroker) at Smith Barney in New York City.

mal classes. During the training, prospective brokers learn about the following:

- Sales techniques, including practice phone calls.
- Laws designed to safeguard the investing public.
- The paper and electronic record keeping that go along with buying or selling an investment.
- The different types of investments offered by the firm.
- The rules for buying "on margin" (when the client borrows part of the investment capital from the AE's firm).
- Formulas for evaluating a company's stock, such as earnings per share (roughly net income divided by the number of common shares owned by the public) and the ratio of a stock's price to its earnings.

Only about half of those who complete the training to be an AE stay in the business for a number of years, and only about one-fourth of those who stay become really successful.

Typical Tasks   Before AEs can make any sales they must acquire clients or customers. At the outset the AE gets customers by making "cold calls," telephoning strangers and asking for business. Names of potential clients may come from membership lists of organizations, such as special interest clubs and alumni associations, or from lists that may be bought. These are usually lists of people likely to have money to invest, such as country club members or owners of boats.

In a typical call the AE gives his or her name and the firm name and then tries to determine what the person's investment goals are. Everyone wants to make money, but some people are more concerned about safety, others want monthly income, some want their investments to grow in value, and still others may be willing to risk a loss in the hope of a larger gain. Finally, the AE asks if he or she may call again with some appropriate advice. Account executives must make many calls before a "prospect" becomes a "customer." In the process, they hear a phone slammed down many times.

To make a sale, the AE must call prospects and established customers with an appropriate investment recommendation. AEs may get some investment ideas from the business press, including such publications as the *Wall Street Journal*, *Barron's*, *Forbes*, *Business Week*, and *Fortune*, but they usually depend on recommendations from analysts in their own firms. The analysts report on various stocks. The AE decides which are most likely to appeal to a particular person. They must always be alert for a client whose situation and investment concerns have changed.

Ethics and Regulations The investment world offers numerous temptations to dishonesty, and over the years many investors have been hurt by unscrupulous brokers. For this reason, stockbrokers are regulated by several private and governmental bodies. Account executives must behave ethically. They cannot make exaggerated claims about a stock or guarantee its performance in the future. Clients' interests and wishes must always be the first concern. Account executives are expected to adhere to the "suitability," or "know your customer," rule. This means that an AE must recommend investments that are appropriate to the situation of the client. It would be unethical for the AE to try to sell a speculative stock to a retired person who needs monthly dividend checks to live on.

It is also unethical, as well as illegal, for AEs to encourage their customers to sell stock too frequently. This process, known as "churning," is an attempt to generate commissions. Account executives also must not engage in unauthorized trading; that is, they may not make purchases or sales that the customer has not previously agreed to.

Account executives must be sure that if they and some customers own the same stock, their customers do better

(continued on page 22)

A DAY IN THE LIFE OF AN ACCOUNT EXECUTIVE

Margaret Kidd, a 24-year-old account executive in the Wall Street office of a major brokerage firm, is one of 2 women out of 20 brokers in her office. While still in college she had worked as a "cold caller" and had sold real estate tax shelters in her native Houston, Texas.

7:30–9:00 A.M.

- Opens the office and reviews file of calls to make that day. The file includes potential clients and "Green Sheets" (names of people who have answered the company's ads and requested information).
- Reviews large file of useful lists, including *Social Register* names in New York City (to be called from the office on Saturday, because only home phone numbers appear) and members of Houston country clubs.
- Searches data on computer and calls the bond trading desk. She is looking especially for municipal bonds (which represent borrowing by city govern-

ment agencies) from Texas that are both safe and will mature (pay back the lenders) in less than three years.

Concentrating in one area—like municipal bonds in the Southwest—and becoming a specialist sets you apart. Clients know I'll tell them about good issues. My firm's bond traders call when they have attractive bonds.

- Attends weekly meeting to hear about a new mutual fund and to practice selling techniques.

9:00–11:00 A.M.

- Makes 20 calls—14 cold calls to doctors in small Texas cities (none are available, so she leaves a toll-free number, her name, the name of her firm, and says she is calling about a short-term municipal bond) and 6 calls to people she has spoken to before. No sales.
- Makes 22 cold calls.
- Does more phone research on Texas municipal bonds.

I don't get discouraged. I don't even think about rejection.

11:00 A.M.–1:00 P.M.

- Opens a new account with sale of five University of Houston bonds to a large investor she has been pursuing for four months.
- Leaves desk to complete paperwork for new account.
- Takes subway and walks up seven flights to the loft of new client, an art-

ist, to pick up a check; returns to office. Payment for this client's purchase is due and Ms. Kidd feared a mail delay.

You get to work with many kinds of people in this business.

1:00–3:00 P.M.
- Makes calls and does paperwork for the artist's new account.
- Makes quick return call to a friend to confirm evening dinner plans.
- Calls a car dealer (car dealers, like doctors, have been targeted as prospects) with whom she has spoken before. Conversation is pleasant, but she is not able to sell an oil exploration stock recommended in a weekly bond report by her firm's analysts.

I try to plan each day to call a variety of people.

- Is annoyed by unnecessary call from operations person who did not read accurately the new account paperwork.
- Completes new account paperwork for artist.
- Makes seven cold calls to Texas doctors and previous contacts in Houston.
- Makes four return calls to prospects.
- Drinks apple juice at desk, for lunch.

If a friend from Texas comes to town, then I might have a real lunch. It doesn't happen often.

3:00–5:00 P.M.
- Opens fourth new account of the day,

for a New York City client who buys five municipal bonds. An assistant helps with the paperwork.
- Calls client who owns the stock praised by analyst this morning to chat about what a good decision that purchase was. Mentions a new investment and sells him 100 shares, then talks casually about other investments.

After I make a sale, I call the client in a few weeks just to chat, to build the relationship. I don't try to make a sale each time I call.

5:00–6:00 P.M.
- Gets a call from hand-me-down client (his broker has left the firm), patiently explains investments for half an hour, but makes no sale.
- Gets call from California client whose recent stock purchase is doing poorly. Although Ms. Kidd would get a commission on a sale, she advises him to hold on until he receives a dividend.

6:10 P.M.
- Leaves the office two hours earlier than usual to go home and make dinner for friends. Although she opened 4 new accounts, making this a good day, she has made only about 65 calls, 135 fewer than on her best days.

I do this because my best skills are not academic. They are selling via the telephone. I like good clothes, gold jewelry, and trips to Europe, and if I'm successful here, I will have them.

(continued from page 19)

than they do. For instance, if the price of the stock is falling and several customers, as well as the AE, want to sell, the customers' shares must be sold first so that they get a higher price than the AE.

Advancement   Account executives can advance by generating a great deal of commission income for their firms. Successful AEs may become executives or officers of the firm, or go into management and supervise other brokers. A manager may have a less hectic work day and the greater financial security of a salary plus bonus, but the loss of commissions is likely to mean a reduction in total income. A third possibility is to become an independent money manager. This is, in effect, a way for AEs to be in business for themselves. This requires passing another examination, but it also means keeping a larger portion of commissions. Independent money managers must pay a fee for executing their transactions to a "clearing" firm that has a seat on the various exchanges. They must also rely on independent securities analysts and other services to replace the investment recommendations and other back-up activities provided to AEs who work within an investment firm.

SALES ASSISTANT

S ales assistant is a support position in the securities industry. The sales assistant backs up one to four AEs by answering customers' questions, mailing out research reports and other materials, helping to route transactions through a firm's operations department, and solving routine problems, such as incorrect entries on a customer's statement. This support frees the AE to spend as much time as possible selling securities.

Advantages and Disadvantages   Sales assistants have the opportunity to learn the securities industry from the inside. They are sponsored by their firms to take the examination that can lead to becoming an AE. The worst aspect of the job is the problem-solving tasks, which may involve dealing with angry customers. The sales assistant position is salaried at a moderate level.

Qualifications, Training, and Advancement   Successful sales assistants must be assertive enough when handling problems so that the problem becomes a priority for the people who can solve it. They should have good telephone personalities and be able to handle many details at once.

Sales assistant is an entry-level position, requiring no prior experience in the industry. To be hired for the job, you must convince recruiters that money is very important to you, and that you want to get into the securities business and are confident and competitive enough to succeed in it. You should have good grades and a bachelor's degree, preferably from a good college. Interviewers also look for evidence of commitment and responsibility, such as having held leadership positions in school activities.

Sales assistants who pass the account executive examination usually move to a similar job in a different firm, often one that is smaller than where they began. There they can take on greater responsibility and handle a greater variety of tasks. After a few years in this second job, a sales assistant usually becomes an AE.

Victoria K. Gahan, a sales assistant at Smith Barney in New York City.

INSTITUTIONAL EQUITIES TRADER

Between 80 and 90 percent of all trading in the stock market is done by institutional investors. These are organizations, such as pension funds, insurance companies, and bank trust departments, that are responsible for investing enormous amounts of money profitably and safely. Because such institutions own large numbers of shares of stock, small price changes in any one stock cause big changes in its value. Therefore, the people who manage the varied investments, or portfolios, of these organizations are extremely active traders.

Several types of traders have institutional investors as clients. Each category handles a different aspect of institutional trading. Because of the quantity of shares and large sums of money involved, all of these traders work in a very high-pressure, high-stakes environment. They must be alert to the slightest sign of news that affects their customers and be as ready to move as athletes in peak condition. They are compensated extremely well for their skill.

Sales Traders   Sales traders function like personal account executives for a small number of institutional investors. Their day starts with an early morning meeting at which they learn what stocks their major customers want to buy or sell, hear evaluations and recommendations of stocks, news of events that might affect the stock market, and reports on stock exchanges around the world. Then they make 50 or more phone calls a day to tell their clients' portfolio managers the latest developments both in the market and with particular stocks. When a client decides to buy or sell, the sales trader sees that the trade is executed either by calling the floor trader directly or working through the firm's position traders. In an investment firm the sales traders sit near position traders in a large room that is buzzing with activity—phones ringing and people shouting, waving arms, and pacing the floor.

Sales traders at several firms compete with each other to gain the preference of an institutional investor's portfolio manager. The quality of a trader's information and recommendations, plus personal compatibility, can secure this relationship. Traders also woo clients by entertaining them, and two or three nights a week the trader's day may end with a business dinner and seeing a show or sports event.

Position Traders Block or position traders buy and sell stocks in quantities (blocks) of 10,000 or more shares. Like sales traders, position traders start the day with a morning meeting and may end it entertaining clients. During the day, however, they have different responsibilities. Position or block traders must make markets for their institutional clients. This means buying up stock to accumulate large blocks in the investment firm's account, so that when an institutional client wants to purchase that stock it is available. In other words, the firm itself can fulfill the client's order to buy or sell (position traders also purchase stock from clients) independently of what other large buyers and sellers are doing.

Each trader is responsible for about 100 stocks of a similar type or industry. The symbols identifying each stock flash on a screen or monitor each time there is a price change. Whenever a purchase is made, the position trader shouts it out to let the sales traders know that the stock is available for sale to their institutional clients. The position trader constantly receives phone calls from sales traders and floor traders announcing shares that are needed and the latest prices, or confirming trades that have been executed.

The position trader, whether sitting at his or her post, or pacing up and down in front of it to release tension, makes 50 to 100 investment decisions an hour. They may base their decisions on an emotional "feel" for a given stock. But they also rely on information from stock ticker tapes, computer monitors, news tapes that flash current events across the room, and from analysts who are monitoring the performance of the entire market.

Floor Traders   Floor traders handle transactions on the floors of the New York, American, and other stock exchanges. They work from locations around the sides of the trading floors to execute the buy and sell orders issued by sales and position traders. As they receive orders, floor traders move around the exchange to learn the latest prices of the stocks in question. To actually execute a trade, the floor trader buys stocks from and sells stocks to various *specialists* on the exchange floor. The floor trader's responsibility to the firm is to get the best price at the time and under the conditions given by the customers. Customers may specify a date or price for the sale or purchase. The New York Stock Exchange is an auction market, and a stock's price is, usually, the figure at which an owner is willing to sell and a buyer is willing to buy the stock. Traders continually monitor a number of financial and current events indicators to see whether they will be able to get a better price later.

Qualifications and Advancement   Successful traders of all types have many qualities in common. They can digest a lot of diverse information quickly and make sense of it. They have a "feel" for the market and use it to make money for clients and for the firm. Major New York firms recruit prospective traders at the country's most prestigious graduate business schools. Typical firms might make offers to 12 out of 200 candidates. They are looking for young men and women who are bright, driven to succeed, perceptive, show evidence of being "workaholics," have good social

Institutional equities traders on the floor of the New York Stock Exchange.

skills, are honest and decisive, and are already knowledgeable about the stock market.

A beginning trader learns about the different trading
areas in the investment firm and then chooses or is chosen
for one. There he or she watches and assists, continually
asking questions and doing whatever is needed. Beginners'
tasks may range from telephoning a floor trader to running
errands. Gradually, beginning traders are given increased
responsibility for placing and initiating trades and having
contact with clients. Finally, after proving their ability to
assume responsibility, they are trusted to commit enormous blocks of money for clients and for their own firms.

BOND TRADER

T he buyer of a bond is lending money to a
corporation or government agency. A bond is
an IOU stating that the company or agency
promises to repay the lender the full amount
of the loan at a specified maturity date, as
well as a fixed rate of interest in the meantime. Bonds
issued by local governments and their agencies are known
as *municipals*.

*Gail S. Dickstein,
a bond broker at
Lebenthal in New
York City.*

The full amount of the loan or bond is known as *par
value*. Bonds are usually issued at $1,000 par value. The
borrower (corporation or government agency) pays a specified amount of interest every year to the bond owner or
lender (the investor), and repays $1,000 for each bond
owned at the maturity date. However, many bonds are sold
by one investor to another before the maturity date. In this
secondary bond market, the price of the bond may be
higher or lower than $1,000 due to fluctuations in interest
rates. When interest rates go up, bond prices go down,
and vice versa. It is this variability and volatility—rapid up
and down movement—of bond prices that makes bond
traders' judgment so important and their days so hectic.

Jonathan Lake (left) and Larry Ansel, bond traders at Lebenthal in New York City.

The bond market is enormous. There are about 1.5 million different municipal bond issues currently outstanding. In 1986 the total value of new issues was about $200 billion. In addition, there are thousands of corporate bond issues and the many billions of dollars' worth of bonds issued by the United States Treasury. The value of U.S. Treasury debt dwarfs the value of all the stocks on the New York Stock Exchange, and three-quarters of all securities traded on the Exchange represent debt, or bonds, as opposed to equity, or stock.

What Bond Traders Do   Bond traders buy and sell outstanding, or previously issued, bonds, and set a price on the bonds with which they are involved. A bond's price is determined by supply and demand for the particular bond. The trader must estimate both the supply of and the demand for the particular bond and then try to get the best price—highest for the seller and lowest for the buyer—for the firm.

Many factors influence the value of a bond, including interest rates; the activity of investors (a lot of buying activity raises bond prices); the availability of other similar bonds; and the "mood" of the market. Traders must be knowledgeable enough to evaluate these and other factors accurately. They must make pricing decisions with split-second timing, often in response to a telephone order to buy or sell at just a slight difference in price. A trader typically spends almost the whole day on the telephone—sometimes on two telephones—with nearby computer screens flashing bond prices and a book giving other bond prices on his or her lap.

Advantages and Disadvantages   Successful bond traders can make a great deal of money, usually receiving a base salary plus a bonus. The bonus typically is based partly on the profitability of the firm or department, and partly on the amount of income the individual trader brings to the firm. An income of more than $100,000 a year is not unusual.

Activity in the bond market has grown enormously in recent years. For this reason, young people can get a great deal of responsibility—committing large amounts of the firm's money—quickly. This provides the potential for making large profits and possibly large losses for the firm. The amount of profit or loss attributed to an individual's activities is the major factor determining that person's success. Politics and personality play a smaller role than in most other work environments.

But there are negatives as well. The pressure is intense. The amounts of money committed at any one time are enormous, and the outcome of a trade can turn on $\frac{2}{32}$ of a dollar. Many traders find that their personal lives suffer because of this pressure. Because of the stress, many people "burn out" early; 40 is "old" for a trader.

Qualifications and Training Successful bond traders have, first of all, a good number sense. They should have a good memory for trades; be able to make decisions quickly and live with them; be able to take criticism and live with losses. Bond traders should be good salespeople; it is, after all, a business of selling.

It is extremely difficult to get a job as a bond trader. At Merrill Lynch, the country's largest brokerage firm, there are 10,000 AEs and only 100 municipal bond traders. A recruiter may see 200 candidates at a top graduate school of business and then make job offers to only 2 of them. Recruiters look for people who have a master's degree in business administration (M.B.A.), usually from a prestigious school; who love and understand the bond market; and an entrepreneurial, risk-taking personality.

Beginners receive on-the-job training by first assisting a trader, then gradually taking responsibility for trades, moving from junior to senior trader as the amount of money entrusted to them increases.

The bond trading floor at Merrill Lynch in New York City.

BOND
TRADER

Another way to start working in a bond trading department is by becoming a *liaison*. This is the middle person between the broker and either the trader who handles or the agency that originates the bond being sold. Liaisons must be good with numbers and know enough about the bonds their firm is selling to describe them accurately to customers and AEs. To get a liaison job, it is necessary to contact someone in a bond department directly; these jobs do not go through recruiters or personnel departments.

SECURITIES ANALYST

James Schainuck, a securities analyst at Ladenburg, Thalmann & Co., Inc.

A securities analyst studies specific securities, estimates their future earnings and *dividends* (payments to stockholders), evaluates them in terms of their current prices, and makes "buy," "sell," or "hold" recommendations. An analyst may specialize in either stocks or bonds. Analysts may work on the "buy side," helping large institutions, such as insurance companies and pension funds, decide how to invest and protect the enormous amounts of money they manage. Or analysts may be on the "sell side," mainly in brokerage firms where they advise AEs about investments to recommend to clients and directly recommend investments to the portfolio managers who are on the "buy side."

A securities analyst becomes an expert in an industry group or groups such as toys, electronics, or automobiles. The analyst studies the companies in the group, trying to assess accurately the potential of a company's stock. In effect the analyst is asking, "In the supply and demand market that sets stock prices, will the demand for this particular stock cause its price to rise or fall, and if so, when and how much?"

To make these decisions, an analyst looks at trends within the company and the industry. Trends in the company or industry might involve labor relations (is a strike likely?), or profitability over the last few years. The analyst also tries to understand what factors are influencing the particular company and industry, and what impact they will have on the stock price. For example, the development of new products, new uses for old products, or new efforts to sell products might increase demand, while an innovative competitor may reduce demand.

To decide on a stock's relative value in the marketplace, an analyst must compute various ratios and indexes. These figures are compared to those of a previous period and projected for a year into the future. The analyst makes similar calculations for the stock's industry and for the market in general. The ratios and indexes for the company are compared to those of the industry, and both are then compared to those for the entire market. The analyst also tries to evaluate the company's *cash flow* (the actual money being received and spent as a company does business) relative to that of other companies in the industry. Finally, the analyst evaluates all of the data and decides whether its stock should be bought, held, or sold, and for what category of investors it should be recommended.

A bond analyst does similar calculations and evaluations for a company's or government agency's projected income and expenditures. The bond analyst must determine whether the organization will be able to meet the schedule of payments for both the interest and principal of its bonds.

An analyst gets some of the information necessary for these calculations from the company or agency itself. Companies must file various formal reports with the Securities and Exchange Commission (SEC), the federal agency that regulates the securities industry. Companies also issue press releases, hold press conferences, and meet with analysts whenever they have information they want investors to know. Analysts also personally contact managers of the companies for which they are responsible to ask about new products and plans for the future.

This primary source (from the company itself) information must be supplemented by secondary source data, such as reports and analyses issued by various investment industry publications. Analysts get additional information from trade group statistics and publications, the company's customers and suppliers, and other analysts. Some information may be biased; a good analyst knows how to evaluate the accuracy and reliability of each source.

After analysts decide on their recommendations, they must convince brokers and investors to act on them. To do this, they must make a strong case by offering clear data to support their predictions. Analysts who have good track records—whose recommendations have proved reliable in the past—are likely to be convincing. An analyst must be able to make good presentations, both in person (more common in a small firm) and in writing (more common in a large firm).

Advantages and Disadvantages   Analysts are well compensated. Starting analysts with M.B.A. degrees and some related work experience make from $30,000 to $50,000 a year or more. Once they become senior analysts, which can take from one to three years, they receive base salaries ranging from $75,000 to $200,000 plus a bonus. In good years the bonus may be as much as the analyst's base salary. A few superstar analysts make $500,000 a year. These salaries are for analysts on the "sell side" of Wall Street, mainly in brokerage firms. Analysts on the "buy side," mainly in insurance companies and pension funds, may receive about 20 percent less.

There are other advantages as well. The work is challenging and intellectually demanding. Analysts make their own decisions about how to gather information and which stocks to recommend, although in many firms they are reviewed by an investment committee. Analysts can be creative by making spoken or written presentations in their own style. They have the power to talk to the top officers of companies and industry leaders and may receive public recognition in newspaper or magazine articles.

There is also a negative side. When the stock market is falling, analysts may have difficulty getting people's attention. (No one wants to communicate or hear bad news.) Some may lose their jobs. Analysts work extremely long hours. They are often making presentations to investors or AEs during the business day, so they must do their research early in the morning or late at night. Travel can take up as much as 30 percent of an analyst's life, and it can be hectic and pressured. A day on the road may start with a breakfast meeting and go through a dinner meeting and evening event. The analyst must be continually alert through it all, day after day if necessary.

Qualifications, Training, and Advancement   It is difficult to get a start as an analyst. Some firms have formal training programs, but most junior analysts are trained by senior analysts. When the market is active, senior analysts do not have time to train new people; when it is slow, no one wants to hire new analysts. Those who are hired usually have an M.B.A. degree.

Some people may be hired as analysts after working for the companies analysts watch. This is most likely for people who work in technical companies, such as those involved with computers, electronics, pharmaceuticals, chemicals, and oil and gas exploration, where expertise is particularly difficult to obtain.

People who have worked as analysts may move into management in their firms. They may become investment bankers or portfolio managers. Some analysts move to jobs in the industries they have been analyzing, where their experience has prepared them to do planning, market evaluation, investor relations, or other financial work.

INVESTMENT BANKER

Investment bankers serve the needs of corporations as they come in contact with securities markets. Corporations use the services of investment bankers when they want to raise money from the public. Investment bankers make arrangements for issuing stocks or bonds and initiate private placements (the sale of securities to a limited group of experienced investors). Corporations will also call on an investment banking firm when they merge with, acquire, or are acquired by other companies.

Although corporate clients often come to investment bankers in such situations, it is more usual for investment bankers to approach corporations with suggestions for new financing or structural arrangements. To make useful suggestions at the right time, investment bankers must know their client companies and potential client companies thoroughly. They must be fully aware of the various financial services and products their own firms offer, and they must have up-to-the-minute information about prices in various financial markets, such as the market for stocks and the market for bonds.

Career Stages In their first two or three years on the job, young investment bankers are likely to be assigned to a team or group handling specific projects. Here they can use their financial training to analyze client companies for the benefit of the team. They visit the companies themselves to verify that the facts stated in reports are accurate and complete. These visits are part of the process called "due diligence," which is required by the SEC to ensure that potential investors receive completely accurate information, negative as well as positive, about a company. The securities laws hold investment bankers responsible for information that is inaccurate or withheld.

In the next career stage, investment bankers are responsible for managing deals or parts of deals, while they begin to specialize in a product or industry. As they become more knowledgeable in their specialties, investment bankers take responsibility for carrying out an entire deal.

Later still, investment bankers market or sell deals and products to clients. Finally, they become senior marketers, whose major responsibility is to propose deals to their clients, leaving the details of execution to junior people. At this stage, investment bankers are usually about 35 years old and have been in the field for about ten years.

Advantages and Disadvantages   Investment bankers have high status and are paid extremely well; in a good year, partners in major firms, many of whom are in their thirties, can earn more than a million dollars. But they may also work such long hours and travel so much that they may not have time to enjoy what they are earning.

The work itself is rewarding. It can be stimulating and creative, challenging and demanding. Investment bankers must take part in tough negotiations and solve difficult problems. They come into contact with varied industries and top executives all over the country and, increasingly, the world.

Then there are the negatives. Investment bankers are always outsiders at the client companies. They may feel frustrated by never being able to learn everything they feel they should know and never being sure when they have provided enough service to a client.

Some aspects of investment banking may be either positive or negative, depending on the individual. These include frequent crises, pressure to perform at peak levels in limited time, and the lack of structure of a field that is changing rapidly. Also on the plus-or-minus list are the competitive environment, both within the firm (where only a few people become partners) and among firms (which compete for the major corporate clients), and being surrounded by people whose main motivation in life is to make money. Some people thrive under these conditions; some will turn away from them.

Qualifications   Good investment bankers combine selling personality with technical expertise. They are also motivated to succeed; risk takers; comfortable about working with numbers; energetic; able to function well under pressure; and good team players.

The best way to become an investment banker is to become a financial analyst (see page 37), perform well at the firm, and then go on to earn an M.B.A. from a prestigious school. The large New York firms recruit investment bankers from the nation's top graduate business schools. At regional firms in such cities as Atlanta, Houston, and San Francisco, holders of M.B.A. degrees from local universities are also considered.

Recruiters—often investment bankers themselves—are looking for M.B.A.s who have studied finance and have usually had some previous work experience in a related field. Other important criteria are a strong academic record and leadership in extracurricular activities. Those selected on campus are usually brought to the firm's offices for several days of interviewing. Students from less prestigious business schools who have strong credentials may be interviewed directly at the firm if they write an outstanding letter stating why they think the field is for them.

Ethical Issues in Investment Banking   The SEC was established in 1934 to regulate the securities industry in order to protect the interests of ordinary investors. SEC regulations, for example, prohibit "insiders" (officers, managers, and anyone with privileged advance information) from trading before information is available to the public. Because a corporation's investment bankers often possess inside information, firms are supposed to keep separate the underwriting and the trading areas of their business. However, where people with different jobs are in frequent close contact, it is often difficult to maintain this separation.

Another ethical issue is full disclosure. The SEC requires that investors and potential investors be given all relevant information about a company. This is accomplished by a type of financial report called a *prospectus*, along with other documents. Copies of all such printed information must be filed with the SEC.

Investment bankers are generally ethical. However, in 1986 and 1987 Wall Street was rocked by a series of insider trading scandals. Several investment bankers who had advance knowledge of stock offerings used that knowledge to buy stock at low prices and make huge profits for themselves and associates. People were indicted, and some, convicted. These events involved behavior that was clearly unethical as well as illegal, and were upsetting to the entire investment community.

FINANCIAL ANALYST

Financial analysts are investment bankers-in-training. This select group of young men and women is hired right out of college to work on Wall Street for two years with the understanding (but no commitment) that at the end of that time they will enter graduate school to get an M.B.A. Because many top business schools accept only students who have had several years of work experience after college graduation, the financial analyst position is a perfect opportunity for those who plan to get an M.B.A.

Financial analysts assist investment bankers by doing research or calculations or performing other tasks as needed. They may have to learn what is happening in capital markets where foreign currencies and government securities are traded, which is information that an investment banker would use to suggest a particular type of money-raising activity to a client. Or they may have to calculate mortgage (real estate interest) rates and income for a real estate investment partnership or provide other numerical data, such as a detailed financial analysis of several companies in a particular industry.

Financial analysts do a great deal of "number crunching," or calculating, usually with a computer. Although most of their work is done behind-the-scenes, financial analysts sometimes get to assist in presentations to clients.

Advantages and Disadvantages   The advantages of being a financial analyst include on-the-job training that can lead to becoming an investment banker, and the chance to learn a lot about finance and thus qualify for positions with other prospective employers. The disadvantages include long hours that interfere with personal life, repetitive tasks, and petty details.

Qualifications and Training   To succeed as a financial analyst, a person should be energetic as well as organized and able to do several things at once. The job calls for close attention to details and quick thinking. A financial analyst must be aggressive enough to get the attention of busy people who have vital information and to request work on interesting and important projects.

Financial analysts, who work almost exclusively in New York City, are recruited from senior classes at prestigious colleges. Of 200 people who might be interviewed on campus, perhaps 8 will survive additional interviews and receive a job offer. Recruiters look for good grades and regular participation in extracurricular activities to show that the candidate is disciplined and capable of honoring a commitment.

THE OPERATIONS DEPARTMENT

There are a variety of jobs to be found in the operations departments of brokerage firms, many of them at entry level. This is the department that handles money, securities, and record keeping. Money moves from the time it is paid by a buyer to a seller, and securities (mainly stock certificates and bonds) move from the seller to the buyer. As the operations department moves the money and securities along, it must record each transaction, make sure that the totals of money and securities match or balance, and that all documents are accurate.

Some of the people who work in the operations department at Lebenthal.

The investment world is a world of services, but only the operations department is devoted exclusively to service. The operations department's accuracy and speed—two qualities that often do not go together—are crucial in keeping customers for the firm.

In one way, buying and selling securities is like buying and selling anything else: money and property of some kind change hands. But in another way it is quite different, and it is this difference that makes the operations department so important. When you buy most items, you can check directly to be sure that the item you take home is the exact one you want and that the price you pay is the one marked on the price tag. If there is something wrong, you can almost always return your purchase—can of beans, red shirt, or refrigerator—for a refund.

With stocks, however, you do not make the purchase directly. Someone else does it for you. Stocks do not have a printed price tag. The price can vary (unless the customer gives an order to buy or sell only at a specific price), depending on the exact moment the purchase is made. Many numbers and symbols accompany a purchase—the customer's account number, the broker's account number, the firm identification, the stock issuer's name, the stock price, and the number of shares purchased. These numbers and letters must all be recorded many times so that the customer, the broker, the stock exchanges, and the regulatory bodies that oversee the industry have accurate records of the transaction. And unlike a red shirt, where the wrong color or size is obvious, with a securities purchase, errors are difficult to trace. A zero left off or added or a decimal point placed incorrectly can mean disaster. More than 90 percent of all transactions are executed without problems.

Routing Transactions in the Operations Department
The work of the operations department begins when an account executive sells stock to a customer. The wire operator at that branch office immediately enters the order into a computer. Because of the huge volume of transactions, investment firms were early users of computers.

After the order has been executed, the operations work moves to the firm's operations center, usually in a less prestigious location than the firm's headquarters. Here the "trade and confirm" or "purchase and sale" area sends confirmation of the trade immediately to both the buyer and the seller, and enters the amount of the AE's commission into the computer. If the customer is new, the trade must first go through the new accounts area where a clerk checks documentation, such as the customer's social security number. Then a clerk compares the information from the buying and selling brokers. If there is a discrepancy, the clerk or the area supervisor must track it down and correct it.

Next the transaction data goes to the cashiers, who are responsible for receiving and delivering securities. They contact the clearing facility, an enormous warehouse where many firms store stock certificates. Stock certificates are usually held in the brokerage firm's vault for safekeeping, instead of being mailed to the customer. This saves time and trouble when the customer wants to sell, but it also means that an error may go undetected for a long time. Clerks at the clearing house transfer the stock to the purchaser's account. If the stock certificate is not to be held by the firm, it is sent through a branch cashier at the branch office and a transfer agent (usually a bank) to the customer. The branch cashier also sends the customer's payment to the firm's central cashier area, where the completed transaction is recorded. After every transaction, the firm's accounts are totaled or balanced so that money on hand matches stocks and bonds sold. Some firms have a separate area, the money desk, to deal with incoming and outgoing payments.

Stock purchasers may borrow a certain percentage of the stock's price from the brokerage. This is called buying "on margin." Stock purchased in this way must pass through the margin department before it goes to the cashiers. Margin clerks record the transaction and continue to monitor the stock's price. If it falls to the point where the borrowed amount represents more than 50 percent of the value of the stock, the margin manager must notify the AE. The customer must then pay more money, to reduce the borrowed amount. If the customer can not or will not do so, the margin manager can "sell out the position," dividing the proceeds to repay the firm both for the amount of the loan and the interest it has earned. Today large brokerages make more money from interest on margin accounts than from commissions on stock trades, so the margin department is important to a firm's success.

Qualifications and Training   Although the various operations jobs perform different functions, they all involve a great deal of telephoning, extensive use of computers and/or calculators, repetitive tasks, speed and accuracy, and dealing with many people. These positions are suited to high school graduates who have an aptitude for numbers and/or keyboard and computer skills. Some firms look for college graduates, who are placed most often as cashiers and margin clerks. Firms also look for some actual work experience as evidence of an applicant's seriousness and knowledge about what is involved in holding a job.

New employees receive on-the-job training in the area for which they are hired, and they may later receive additional training that will help them move ahead in that area or move to another area within the operations department. Firms also may pay for beginning workers to take outside courses, such as those run by the Securities Industry Association, from which they can learn about the entire industry.

The trading floor of the New York Stock Exchange.

Advantages and Disadvantages   Operations is a growing area with opportunities for advancement. It is a good area for high school graduates who have bookkeeping, typing, telephone, and computer skills. Operations is not for someone who does not like pressure and does not want to work long hours. It is also not for someone who gets bored easily by doing repetitive tasks.

Advancement   A person who is successful in operations jobs has capabilities that are useful throughout the industry: working long hours under pressure, identifying and solving problems, having an eye for detail, requesting and assuming additional responsibility, and working well with others.

In the past, the operations department was viewed as a route into sales or trading. Today, except for those who get a college degree, that is unlikely. However, people who are successful in operations will hold a variety of positions there and can become managers. Operations management positions are more responsible and challenging, and can pay more than $100,000 when the stock market is doing well. Nonmanagers can earn $35,000 to $50,000 a year after about 10 years in the field.

PREPARING FOR AN INVESTMENT CAREER

Even in high school, it is not too early to take steps that will make you attractive to recruiters. Some of the things you can do are the following:

1. Read articles and books about investing and the world of Wall Street. Keep a file of articles that interest you.
2. Choose a stock and invest in it, either with actual money or on paper. Follow your stock over a period of time.
3. Become a leader in at least one extracurricular activity and participate in athletic activities at your school. Recruiters see these experiences as evidence of persuasive ability, commitment, and teamwork.
4. Keep a list of people who might help you when you look for a job. These can be neighbors, friends of your family, companies that sponsor extracurricular activities, or graduates of your high school or college.
5. Take a summer or after-school job in an investment firm. Brokerages hire young people to be "cold callers" and make the preliminary phone contacts with potential clients. There are also jobs in file and mail rooms, and as messengers or secretaries. If you have computer or typing skills, try to get work in an operations department. Get job leads from people you or your family may know, or inquire at personnel departments.

Before you apply for a job with any investment firm, find out what you can about the company's reputation. Talk to people who work there or have dealt with the firm, or with people from similar companies.

GLOSSARY

account executive (AE), stockbroker An agent who acts as an intermediary between buyers and sellers of *investments*.

American Stock Exchange (AMEX) One of the major U.S. stock markets.

bond A certificate that represents a loan to a company or government agency. The issuing company (the borrower) pays interest for the use of the money and must repay the entire amount of the bond at a specified time.

bond trader A person who acts as an intermediary between buyers and sellers of already *issued bonds*.

boutique A small, specialized *brokerage* or *investment banking firm* that researches *securities*.

brokerage, brokerage firm, or investment firm An organization that facilitates the buying and selling of stocks and other types of *investments*. *Account executives* are employed by investment firms.

cash flow The actual money received by a company as a result of its operations and available to the company for spending.

corporation One of the legal forms in which a business can be established. The people who own the business are able to act as one; each is financially responsible only up to the amount he or she originally invested.

commercial bank A state or federally chartered institution that accepts checking accounts, makes business loans, and performs a variety of other financial services. It cannot *underwrite* stock *issues*.

commission A fee paid to an agent for a business transaction, usually figured as a percentage of the dollar value of the transaction.

dividend A portion of a company's earnings that is distributed to stockholders; the amount is determined by the board of directors.

financial analyst A person who does research to determine whether it is advisable to invest in a company or industry.

floor trader A person who buys and sells equities directly on the floor of the stock exchange.

institutional investor An organization such as a *pension fund* or *insurance company* that invests large amounts of money in *securities*.

insurance company An organization that receives money in the form of premiums paid by individuals or organizations, and is obligated to pay a specified amount to the insured if a specified misfortune occurs. Insurance companies are typical *institutional investors*.

interest rate Money paid by a borrower to a lender in return for the use of money, usually a fixed percentage of the amount borrowed.

investment Property acquired for the purpose of gaining future income. Purchased stocks are an investment. Also, placing money with an organization with the aim of realizing a profit.

investment banker A person who arranges company financing through the *issue* of new *stocks* and *bonds*.

investment banking firm An organization that helps companies raise money by *underwriting* new *stock* and *bond issues*.

issue The offer of a company's *securities* for sale; the sale of a company's securities. Also, the actual shares being sold.

liaison A person employed in a bond trading department who serves as an intermediary between an *account executive* and a *bond trader* or the company that is *issuing* a *bond*.

municipal A *bond* issued by a local government agency.

mutual fund Shares in an investment company that pools its shareholders' money in order to invest in the *stocks* and *bonds* of a variety of other organizations.

NASDAQ (pronounced "nazdak") The computerized National Association of Securities Dealers Automatic Quotation network that provides price quotations on *stocks* traded *over-the-counter*.

New York Stock Exchange (NYSE) The major U.S. market where *shares of stock* are traded.

operations department The service segment of a *brokerage firm* that handles record keeping and transfers of money and stock certificates when *stocks* and *bonds* are traded.

over-the-counter market (OTC) The nationwide network of brokers who handle transactions of *stocks* that are not listed on an exchange.

par value The stated amount or face value of a *stock* or *bond*.

payout The direct payment of a *commission*.

pension fund Money to be invested paid by members of an organization such as a union or company; it is expected that the investments will increase in value to provide retirement income for the contributors. ·

position trader, block trader An *institutional equities trader* who buys large quantities of *stocks* so that a *brokerage* will have them available for purchase by an institutional client.

principal The original or total amount of a loan; the face value of a *bond*.

sales assistant A person who performs support activities for one or more *account executives* in an *investment firm*.

sales trader An *institutional equities trader* who buys and sells *stocks* on behalf of *institutional investors*.

securities *Stock* certificates or *bonds* that are evidence of property or debt.

securities analyst A person who researches the companies issuing *stocks* and *bonds* to assess their future potential and makes trading recommendations.

Securities and Exchange Commission (SEC) A U.S. government agency established by Congress in 1934 to regulate the trading of *stocks* and *bonds* to protect investors.

share of stock Any of the equal parts into which the entire value, or equity, of a company is divided. It represents part ownership in the company.

specialist A *stockbroker* who handles specific *securities* on the floor of a stock exchange. The specialist seeks to maintain a fair and orderly market for the *stocks* to which he or she is assigned.

stock market The exchange or marketplace where *stocks* and *bonds* are traded.

supply and demand The relationship between the price, quantity available, and demand for an item or service, including *shares of stock*. When demand is high and supply is low, people are willing to pay more.

underwriting The process of buying newly *issued securities* from a *corporation* and reselling them to the public. *Investment banking firms* underwrite new *issues*.

Wall Street The street in lower Manhattan, New York City, where the *New York* and *American Stock Exchanges* are located; considered the major financial center of the United States. Also, refers generically to the investment industry.

FURTHER READING

Calhoun, Mary E. *How to Get the Hot Jobs in Business and Finance*. New York: Perennial Library (Harper & Row), 1986. Hard-hitting job-hunting recommendations and detailed information about various workplaces in the financial world.

Career Associations. *Career Choices for Undergraduates Considering an M.B.A.* New York: Walker and Company, 1985. Eight major industries are explained, including investment banking and securities. Discussion of interviews ends each chapter.

Epstein, Rachel S., and Nina Liebman. *Biz Speak: A Dictionary of Business Terms, Slang and Jargon*. New York: Franklin Watts (Grolier), 1986. The language of the investment world, from the board rooms to the back rooms.

Prashker, Marti, and Peter S. Valiunas. *Money Jobs!* New York: Crown Publishers, Inc.: 1983. A valuable guide to financial training programs that lead to high-level positions in the investment, accounting, banking, and insurance fields.

Sherman, Stratford P. "Why the Youngsters' Party May Be Ending." *Fortune*, November 24, 1986, pp. 29–40. Describes the cyclical nature of Wall Street and its impact on investment bankers.

"The All-America Research Team." *Institutional Investor*. Annual feature of every October issue. Survey with profiles of the year's best-performing securities analysts specializing in various industries. Must reading for prospective analysts.

INDEX

RACHEL S. EPSTEIN, a free-lance writer specializing in business subjects, holds an M.B.A. from New York University. Her articles have appeared in the *Wall Street Journal*, the *Washington Post, Working Woman,* and *Ms.* She is the coauthor also of *Biz Speak: A Dictionary of Business Terms, Slang and Jargon.*

PAUL A. SAMUELSON, senior editorial consultant, is Institute Professor Emeritus at the Massachusetts Institute of Technology. He is author (now coauthor) of the best-selling textbook *Economics.* He served as an adviser to President John F. Kennedy and in 1970 was the first American to win the Nobel Prize in economics.

SHAWN PATRICK BURKE, consulting editor, is a securities analyst with Standard & Poor's Corporation. He has been an internal consultant in industry as well as for a Wall Street investment firm, and he has extensive experience in computer-generated financial modeling and analysis.

ACKNOWLEDGMENTS Page 8, 42, Ed Topple/New York Stock Exchange Archives; 11, Nancy J. Pierce/Photo Researchers, Inc.; 12, UPI/Bettmann Newsphotos; 13, Reuters/Bettmann Newsphotos; 14, photograph by Dana Duke; 18, 20, 23, 27, 28, 30, 39, photographs by Mark Ferri; 26, Richard Laird/Freelance Photographer's Guild; 29, Arthur Krasinsky, KPI Inc.

Cover: photograph by George Haling.